Household
HINTS & TIPS

Household
HINTS & TIPS

Lucy Doncaster

igloo

This book was first published in 2004 in Great Britain
by Igloo Books Ltd., Henson Way, Telford Way Industrial Estate,
Kettering, Northants NN16 8PX
info@igloo-books.com

This book was created for Igloo Books
by Amazon Publishing Ltd., 7 Old Lodge Place, Twickenham,
Middlesex, TW1 1QR

Author Lucy Doncaster
Editor Mary Davies
Designer Maggie Aldred

ISBN 1-84561-017-2
Printed and bound in China

Foreword

My fascination with housekeeping history originated in my childhood, when my grandmother used to speak of the traditional methods used by her generation, often referring to her Mrs Beeton 'bible'. This has led to the compilation of this book, containing all of the titbits of household wisdom she passed on, supplemented by leafing through old books, visiting numerous internet sites, scouring the newspapers and probing family members and friends for choice snippets. I hope this book will inspire readers to try out some alternative techniques rather than relying on chemical products alone. I have aimed to integrate traditional tips with modern methods, in order to offer a range of hints which are accessible to all ages and households. Please note, it is important that due caution is taken when using chemicals, products and techniques outlined in this book, and their success cannot be guaranteed. All treatments should be tested prior to application, in an inconspicuous place, and please read and follow all information on product labels with care.

Contents

Stain Removal

Stains occur in every household, and, if left untreated, can be a permanent reminder of dinner parties, sporting accidents or muddy walks past. So try these spot-on solutions to leave your laundry, shoes upholstery and carpets as unblemished as your reputation.

First Aid

Different stains require different treatments according to the type of the fabric, but here are some general points about the immediate action you should take.

The quicker you deal with stains the better. The first step should always be to try and absorb as much of the fluid, or remove as much of the substance, as possible.

If the fabric is dry-clean only, you should rub the stain immediately with an ice cube rather than a cloth as this prevents the stain from setting and avoids damaging delicate fibres.

Wherever possible, try to deal with stains on the reverse of the fabric to prevent them sinking in further. You should always work the solution towards the centre to prevent it spreading.

Salt absorbs stains and is often the best immediate action to take on spills such as red wine and beetroot.

You should never use warm water to treat protein stains, such as egg or blood, as heat will seal in the stain.

If the fabric is washable, check the label to see what temperature the material can withstand.

Clothes

**It is often hard to avoid getting stains on clothes, and
children in particular are prone to picking up a variety
of different marks, ranging from grass, chocolate and grease
to ink, blood and paint. Here are some handy ways to
erase the tell-tale marks of everyday accidents.**

Acrylic paint

Rub the area with soap and cold water,
and then again with methylated spirit, before washing as usual.

Beetroot

Cover the area repeatedly with salt or press the stain between
two slices of dampened bread until all of the fluid is absorbed.
Alternatively, plunge clothes immediately into cold water before
rubbing with liquid detergent. If it is a material like cotton
which won't be spoilt by heat, douse the area with boiling
water until it runs clear.

Blood

Put the garment into a bucket of cold salty water or a solution of
hydrogen peroxide and water in a ration of 1:3 as quickly as possible.
If the blood has dried, then remove any 'crusting' and soak
in cold water with biological detergent before washing as usual.

Chewing gum

Put the article in the freezer for an hour, crack the gum off,
rub the mark with distilled vinegar or egg white, and wash.

Chocolate, coffee and cocoa

For non-delicates, stretch the fabric taut over a bowl, sprinkle
with borax powder and pour boiling water through the stain.
Then soak the item in the solution for an hour before washing.
For more delicate materials, dab the mark with glycerine and leave
for 15 minutes before washing according to recommendations
on the label.

Curry
Hold the stain under warm running water until the
water runs clear, then dab with glycerine and leave overnight
before soaking in biological detergent and washing.

Deodorant
Make a paste of bicarbonate of soda, salt and water
or some glycerine, apply to the affected area
and leave for 15 minutes. Then soak in biological detergent
and water and finally wash.

Fat/grease
Remove as much of the substance as possible, then
carefully blot the area with kitchen towel or brown paper.
Apply baking soda or talcum powder to draw up the grease
and leave for 10 minutes before applying some spray lubricant, such as
WD40, followed 10 minutes later by washing-up liquid. Then wash.

Foundation
Dab with liquid detergent and then rinse.

Fruit juice

Blot the area with kitchen paper to absorb as
much of the stain as possible. If the item is not silk, soak in lemon
juice for 30 minutes and then launder as usual. For silk, blot dry, then
sponge on some distilled vinegar, rinse with cool water and dry-clean.

Grass

Rub nylon with glycerine and leave for an hour before
laundering. For other materials, use methylated spirits and then
rinse with warm water before washing.

Hair dye

Put the item straight into cold water, and then rub with
liquid detergent followed by distilled vinegar.

Ink

The quickest and easiest way to remove ink blotches is to
coat the area in hairspray and let it dry before laundering.
Alternatively, you can rub the spots with a cut lemon and sprinkle
with salt, or rub in a paste made from milk and baking soda
before rinsing and washing.

Lipstick

Rub with methylated spirits, glycerine or petroleum jelly before washing in a 20:1 solution of liquid detergent and ammonia.

Perfume

Rub the area with a 1:1 dilution of water and glycerine before rinsing and laundering as usual.

Perspiration

For recent stains, soak the item in 2.5ml ammonia with 1 litre warm water for half an hour, or apply a paste of baking soda and water and leave overnight. On older stains, dab with neat distilled vinegar and leave for 2 hours.

Plasticine ™

Rub with a clean cloth and lighter fuel and then wash in hot water, or warm water if the garment is made from a delicate material.

Red wine

Apply salt repeatedly until it no longer absorbs wine, or cover the area with white wine, before washing as usual.

Rust

Cover the area with salt and add a few drops of
lemon juice. Leave it for half an hour, preferably in the sun,
and then rinse in a solution of 25ml ammonia
per 10 litres of water before washing.

Salad dressing/mayonnaise

Rub with glycerine and then wash in a mild solution of
25ml ammonia and 10 litres of warm water.

Scorch marks

To remove from white fabric, dampen a clean
cloth with hydrogen peroxide and place it over
the stain, put another clean cloth over the top and
gently warm with an iron.

Tea

For recent spills, soak in a solution of 500ml warm
water and 15ml borax. For older spills, try rubbing with
glycerine or methylated spirits.

Urine

Soak the item in a 6:1 dilution of water and
hydrogen peroxide, with a few drops of ammonia
added. Launder as normal.

White wine

Cover in salt until all the liquid is absorbed and then rinse
with cold water before washing as instructed.

Water-based paint

Rinse in cold water or dab with neat ammonia
before washing.

Carpets and Upholstery

**Carpets and upholstery undergo a lot of wear
and tear, and have to withstand all manner of spills
and accidents. Here are some on-the-spot
suggestions to help banish the blots.**

Burns

Use fine sandpaper to remove most of the burnt fibres and then
trim away any remaining with nail scissors. If it is a carpet burn
in an obvious place, trim some fibres (or a square of carpet if the burn
is large) from a patch of carpet which is hidden, for example by a
piece of furniture, and glue into the hole.

Faded colour

Scatter a mixture of tea leaves and salt over the carpet
before vacuuming.

Grease spots

On rugs, rub with a 1:4 dilution of salt and alcohol.
Alternatively, treat the area with paint thinner or lighter fuel,
and then blot, rather than rub, with kitchen paper.

Maintenance

Regular hoovering helps to maintain the condition of your
carpets as well as improving the appearance of the room.
Vacuum the upholstery once a fortnight too, and try to keep it
out of direct sunlight as this fades the colours.

Mildew or mould

Lightly spray porous upholstery fabric with a 1:1 solution
of tea tree oil and water and then air as much as possible.
If the material is non-porous, use borax or vinegar
instead of tea tree oil.

Muddy patches

Freshen discoloured areas on carpets by
rinsing with water left over from boiling potatoes.

Odours

Sprinkle the carpet with bicarbonate of soda and leave
for 30 minutes before vacuuming.

Rust marks

On carpets and rugs, treat the area with a 1:4 solution of salt and alcohol, rubbing in the direction of the nap.

Scorch marks

Rub the area with a raw onion or potato.

Spills

Salt soaks up most spills – in particular red wine and ink. Apply salt repeatedly until it won't absorb any more liquid, before letting it dry and vacuuming.

Stains

On dark-coloured carpets, rub ground coffee into the affected area before vacuuming.

Treat stubborn stains by gently scrubbing the area with shaving cream and a scrubbing brush after blotting with paper towels.

Shoes

**Shoes and trainers inevitably become scuffed and
dirty, and if left untreated can look scruffy.
Luckily, there are many effective ways to produce
smart results that can help to prolong life too.**

Black marks
Rub with nail polish remover or lighter fuel.

Have a banana
Rubbing leather shoes with the soft inside of a banana skin
cleans and polishes at the same time.

Instant shine
In a hurry? Rub your leather shoes with a baby-wipe. But don't
do this too often as baby-wipes can dry the leather out. Be sure to
clean and polish the shoes properly soon afterwards.

Mud

Leave shoes or trainers on a piece of newspaper outside or
in an airing cupboard before scraping off the worst of the dirt.
It's so much easier to remove once dry.

Odours

Chop the toe off an old pair of tights and fill it with
cat litter, baking soda or tea leaves. Place in the offending
shoes when they are not in use.

Patent leather

Store shoes in a warm place and rub with milk or olive oil
every once in a while to prevent cracking.

Scuffs

For a smooth, unblemished surface, fill scratches and scuffs by
rubbing a raw potato over the affected area before applying polish.

Suede

Rub with a little lemon juice, steam for a few seconds over
a kettle and then brush with a suede brush. A pencil eraser will
remove grease marks.

Waterproofing

For leather, apply a thin, even coat of castor oil.

Wet shoes

Place chopped conkers in saturated shoes – it dries them out.

White leather

Apply cleansing milk with cotton wool before buffing
with a soft cloth.

Laundry

Have your whites lost their glow? Does the thought of washing

your woollens or starching you shirts fill you with horror?

Fear no longer — these laundry lifesavers will make drying

a doddle and washday a breeze.

Caring For Woollens

**Delicate woollens require special treatment,
so try these skin-friendly tips to ensure safe
washing for soft woollens.**

Always use lukewarm water when washing delicate woollens.
Extreme temperatures shock the fibres and can cause
them to shrink.

For extra-soft woollens, add a little distilled vinegar to
the final rinse. It helps to wash out every last trace of soap.

When handwashing, avoid dunking the garment in
and out of the water as this stretches the wool, and press in a
towel to remove excess water rather than wringing.

Hair shampoo and conditioner can be used to clean and
condition delicate fibres such as mohair, angora and cashmere.
Add a small blob of conditioner to the final rinse,
after hand washing with shampoo, and it will help to untangle
matted fibres and soften the fabric, as well as preventing static
and gently perfuming the garment. These products are particularly
suitable for those with sensitive skin – what is suitable
for the scalp, should be suitable for the rest of the body.

If you don't have time to handwash delicates such as cashmere,
it's good idea to put them into a net bag or pillow case with the end
tied up. This prevents them snagging in the washing machine.

To avoid peg marks when you hang less delicate woollens on the line,
try threading an old pair of tights through the sleeves and pegging
that to the line, rather than the actual garment.

If you have a snag in a woollen garment, pull the loop
through to the inside with a sewing or knitting
needle (depending on the chunkiness of the wool).
Never cut the loop as this will cause
the stitches to unravel.

Rubbing matted mohair with a piece of Velcro™ will
restore a garment to its former fluffiness.

Use hair conditioner to restore shape to clothes
which have shrunk. Simply soak the article in a solution of warm
water and conditioner for 30 minutes, before gently stretching
and reshaping while damp.

Blinding Whites

**Clean, crisp, bright whites are always a pleasure
to wear, so here are some easy ways to restore your
laundry to its brilliant best.**

For dazzling whites, try mixing a teaspoon of baking soda
with your washing powder before you put it in the machine.
This also helps to eliminate lingering tobacco odours.

Add a mixture of 1 tablespoon methylated spirit and
1 tablespoon turpentine to the final rinse of your wash to
prevent whites yellowing.

Place a linen bag containing crushed egg shells in your machine
with the load to help whiten the grubbiest garments.

Lemon is a natural bleaching agent and can be used on
most white fabrics apart from silk. Soak the soiled item in a
bucket of boiling water mixed with 100ml (3^1/$_2$ fl.oz) of lemon juice
or a few slices of lemon for at least 30 minutes and then
launder as normal.

Make a delicate bleach solution suitable for whitening woollens by
mixing 3% hydrogen peroxide with water, at a dilution of 1:8.

Line-drying sheets and other white linens on a sunny day
not only freshens but also brightens them.

...and to keep whites white

Test new coloureds for fastness by soaking a small area with warm
water and squeezing. If the dye runs, it's best to wash the garment
on its own. And remember: always wash pale
and dark colours separately.

Line-Fresh Linen

Fresh linen straight from the line has a wonderful scent, but unfortunately this rarely lasts, so try these simple tricks to maintain the freshness long beyond laundry day.

To add a hint of your favourite perfume to your underwear, put a few drops to the final rinse.

When washing a blanket, add a bath cube or a few drops of essential oil to the final rinse for lasting scent. This is particularly effective when the blankets have not been used for a while.

Lightly fragrance your clothes by misting them with a lavender and water solution before you iron them.

Old handkerchiefs can quickly be turned into scent pouches
for chests and drawers by placing some of your favourite aromatic
herbs and flowers, such as lavender or rosemary, in the centre,
before twisting and tying with a ribbon.

Fabric-conditioning sheets are obtainable from most
supermarkets. Used ones, placed in chests and drawers,
help to maintain freshness.

Starching and Ironing

Crisp collars and cuffs are always a confidence booster, and careful starching and ironing improves the appearance of any fabric, especially if it has become limp through multiple washes. But did you know starch also helps to repel dirt and grime? These tips will help you to steam through your ironing with ease.

Add starch to the final cycle of your wash to avoid the hassle of applying starch to each article individually.

Iron collars from the points inwards. It helps to prevent rucking and creasing.

Don't let the iron become too hot when pressing a starched item. It can cause the starch to flake off.

You can make your own starch by mixing 2 teaspoons
of cornstarch with 1 litre of water. Put it in a spray
bottle and use while ironing.

If you accidentally iron-in a crease, simply dab the area with a damp
sponge or spray with some water and iron smooth.

Steam vents on irons can become blocked, especially if you
use starch frequently. Try filling the iron with distilled vinegar and
either switch it on and leave for 20 minutes or press the steam
function repeatedly until the nozzles are clear. Then disconnect
the iron, tip away any remaining vinegar and rinse out.

Don't iron fabric while it's wet enough to cause the iron to hiss. It may result in scorching.

To get rid of grease marks around collars and cuffs, rub the areas with a stick of chalk and leave overnight before washing.

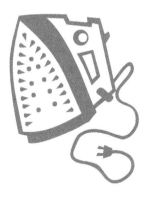

Kitchen

Are you tired of the endless cycle of soak and scrub?

Are you unknowingly aiding and abetting dangerous germs?

Kitchens are areas which require constant attention, so here

are some tidy tricks to ensure a squeaky clean sheen.

Useful Utensils

With the bewildering amount of gadgets on sale it is easy to spend money on unnecessary and expensive items which create clutter. Here are some useful ways to get the same result using existing, everyday kitchen implements.

Ceramic baking beans are not particularly expensive, but if you are not going to use them very often then dried beans or rice work just as well.

A hand-held beater mashes potatoes much better than individual potato mashers and can be used for many more purposes besides.

An ordinary new paint brush is just as good as a 'pastry brush' and will probably be cheaper.

Kitchen paper or a clean tea towel are more effective for drying off rinsed salad leaves than a cumbersome salad spinner.

The plastic tubs that takeaway curries and ready-made sauces come in make very effective storage tubs, especially for freezing and storing smaller quantities. Because they may not be airtight, it's better not to use them for biscuits and cakes. NB Do not put in the oven and always check whether they are suitable for the microwave.

Wearing washing-up gloves, or placing an elastic band around the lid, to open a stiff jar works just as well as a jar-opening gadget.

To keep the inside of your kettle clean, drop in an old oyster shell which will prevent limescale building up.

Egg slicers can be used to cut mushrooms and soft fruits, such as kiwi, strawberries and bananas.

You can easily make café-quality frothy milk for cappuccinos and hot chocolate at home without an expensive gadget. Simply heat the milk in a pan and whisk with a hand-held beater.

Pristine Pans

We all know how frustrating it can be when stubbon stains refuse to shift, so here are some environmentally friendly ways to keep your pans gleaming.

Never put uncoated aluminium pans in a dishwasher.
The metal will react with the detergent and tarnish.

Restore stained copper pots and pans to their
spotless best by dipping half a lemon in salt and rubbing
the marks with a circular motion.

Remove black tarnish from aluminium or stainless steel
cookware by covering the base of the pan with slices of lemon
and water and boiling for 30 minutes.

For badly burned-on food, soak in water for an
hour, and then boil with a chopped onion and a tablespoon of
salt for another hour.

Another good method to try for severe burnt-on stains, is to boil
a solution of 1 litre of water and 1 tablespoon of biological detergent
in the pan for 10 minutes.

Remove hard-water marks from stainless steel pans by
bringing some water and 4 tablespoons of distilled vinegar to
the boil in them, and then cleaning with a nylon scourer.

Don't be tempted to plunge very hot cookware into
water to make cleaning easier. Cookware can warp if it is too
hot when you wash it, so leave it to cool for 10 minutes.

Never use metal implements or wire wool on non-stick coating
– even to remove burnt-on grime. Instead, bring 125ml water and
2 tablespoons of baking soda up to the boil in the pan, then rinse
and dry thoroughly. Alternatively, use a nylon scrubbing brush or pad.

To lengthen the life of a non-stick coating, 'season' the pan
after drying by wiping the inside with some vegetable or olive oil.

To prevent non-stick cookware from becoming scratched
while stacked, place old plastic yoghurt or cream pot
lids between each pan after drying.

Spotless Surfaces

**Kitchen surfaces can be breeding grounds
for bacteria and need regular wiping, but sometimes
conventional cleaning just doesn't leave them
pristine. Here are some other ways to achieve
the cleanest sheen.**

Sterilise your sponges and avoid spreading germs when
wiping surfaces by putting them through the dishwasher
with the day's load.

To lift stains from formica surfaces, cover the area with
lemon juice and leave for 30 minutes before rubbing with
bicarbonate of soda and wiping clean.

Keep wooden surfaces clean by scrubbing with scouring powder
before rubbing in a little olive oil to build up a seal.

Use silicone furniture polish on wooden surfaces in the kitchen rather than wax, which traps grease and softens the surface.

Rub a little non-gel toothpaste onto a plastic worksurface before buffing with a soft cloth to ensure a gleamingly clean result.

To remove rust and water spots from stainless-steel sinks, apply distilled vinegar or alcohol with a sponge or soft cloth.

Rejuvenate dull sinks by wetting paper towels with bleach, pressing them onto the affected surface and leaving for a couple of hours. Then rinse thoroughly.

Clean Cookers and Hobs

Spills are an almost inevitable part of cooking, but they can be tricky to shift and leave your cooker and hob smoking and looking dirty. Try these traditional techniques instead.

Pour salt over recent liquid spills while the oven is on to prevent smoking. When it is turned off and cool, you'll be able to lift the spill easily.

To prevent food from sticking to your cooker top when pans spill over, try rubbing some car wax or distilled vinegar on the surface occasionally after cleaning.

Place a saucer of water containing a few drops of distilled vinegar in the microwave and turn it on for 2 minutes. It will help to remove cooked-on spills and deodorize at the same time.

Remove melted plastic from a hob or oven top by letting it cool and harden before you apply nail-varnish remover. Leave for 10 minutes and then wipe off with a soft, dry cloth.

Clear blocked vents on gas hobs quickly and easily with a pipe cleaner dipped in washing-up liquid.

Use a disposable razor to lift crusty spills and you won't scratch the surface.

Remove marks on stainless-steel ovens with a little baby oil.

Don't want to use chemical solvents on your oven? Try using a 1:4 mixture of borax and baking soda as scouring powder.

To get rid of the smell of a commercial oven-cleaner, put half a lemon in a hot oven and leave for 15 minutes with the door shut, followed by 10 minutes with the door ajar.

To remove burnt-on food stains from a cooker, soak any removable parts overnight in a solution of warm water and biological washing detergent, or mix the same ingredients into a paste and apply directly to the surface.

Tackle heavy, greasy soiling on your cooker top or oven by applying full-strength ammonia to the area, covering with foil and leaving it for as long as possible with the extractor fan on or the windows open. To deal with the inside of the oven, simply leave a cup containing 1ml ammonia and 50ml water overnight, with the oven on its lowest temperature setting. Remember you must wear rubber gloves and keep pets and children away when dealing with ammonia.

Cupboards and Floors

Hygiene is vital in the kitchen, and while most people wipe surfaces regularly, floors and cupboards can often be overlooked. Here are some effective ways to combat grimy floors and sticky shelves.

Loose vinyl floor tiles in the kitchen are both a hazard and a haven for breeding bacteria. If the tiles are undamaged, gently heat them with a warm iron to melt the glue – you'll need the iron set to synthetics and a folded cloth to protect the surface. Lift the tiles, and scrape the old adhesive off the floor before applying fresh glue to the tiles and replacing. If the tiles are damaged, you'll need to put new ones down.

To ensure that the cloth you use to clean floors or shelves is sterile, and avoid spreading germs, put the dampened cloth into the microwave for 1 minute on full power.

Remove black scuffmarks from a white vinyl floor with a pencil rubber, or try rubbing the marks with toothpaste.

Banish stains from lino with very fine wire wool and turpentine, before polishing with a 1:1 mixture of milk and water.

When cleaning a vinyl floor, always sweep or hoover the area first, before mopping with a weak solution of warm water and borax or distilled vinegar to maintain shine as you clean.

Add some bicarbonate of soda to your bucket of hot
soapy water when cleaning the floor or cupboards. This will help
to shift the greasiest of grime.

If your wooden floorboards are creaking, dust some
talcum powder over the joins.

If you have a wooden kitchen floor, add a couple of
teabags to warm water and wipe the surface with a mop dampened
with the solution. This not only cleans but also disguises
scratches and flaws.

Rather than spending ages scrubbing the insides of cupboards, line
them with old newspaper. Then all you have to do is simply discard
the old paper and lay down fresh sheets.

Store bags of sugar and flour in outer plastic bags, or empty them into sealed jars rather than keeping them just in their original wrappings. This helps to ensure that cupboard surfaces don't become sticky or dusty. Keeping sugary items in sealed containers also helps to prevent insects being attracted to the kitchen.

The bottom of pans and baking trays can become greasy if the oven and hobs are not cleaned regularly. To avoid transferring the grime from cooker to cupboard, or from the bottom of one pan to the inside of another if they are stacked, make sure you wash the bottoms of pans as carefully as the insides.

Cupboard and drawer handles are breeding grounds for germs because bacteria is transferred from our hands to them whenever we use them. Include them in your regular cleaning regime and wipe with disinfectant every time you clean the surfaces.

Around the Home

Homes can house all manner of grime, pests, smells and mess, all of

which draw the eye and damage the appearance, ambience and often

the sanitation of the area. Wherever you are in the home, try these

easy ways to defy the dust, prevent the pest and outwit the odour.

Natural Pest Prevention

**Ants, silverfish, flies and mice are just some of
the pests found in the kitchen, and they need to be dealt
with quickly and efficiently. But some modern methods
involve highly toxic ingredients not suitable for a
kitchen, especially if you have pets or children, so here
are some safer alternatives.**

If you don't want to use ant poison in the kitchen,
try dusting cinnamon or black pepper around the area where
the ants are entering your home. Chalk can also act as a deterrent so
draw a line across access points. Alternatively, ants are know to be
deterred by mint. Grow it near doorways or place a
few crushed leaves in entrances.

Are you unlucky enough to have a cockroach problem?
Place jam lids containing a mixture of sugar and borax in a 3:1 ratio
under sinks and behind the fridge, and sprinkle the mixture into
crevices which cannot be accessed by pets or small children.

Mosquitos breed around standing water so make sure it
can't collect anywhere just outside your home. If that's not the cause,
stick some cloves into a lemon and leave it near each window,
or put a saucer of clove oil in every room.

If your pet has fleas, put a couple of mothballs
in the bag of your vacuum cleaner – or dust-collection bin if your
machine is bagless – and vacuum daily for a week.
Then sprinkle garlic powder or iodized salt onto surfaces to kill any
fleas which may be lurking in your carpets or upholstery as well
as treating the animal by conventional means.

Hairspray is an effective and less toxic way of deterring flies
and bees than conventional insect sprays.

Lavender acts as both a deterrent to winged insects and as
a pleasant aroma in the home. Grow it just outside windows, keep
dried lavender in a bowl near windows, or use lavender
oil above an oil burner.

Basil and marigolds will deter winged insects and fleas,
and sprigs of fresh peppermint or camomile will deter mice, so keep
pots on windowsills or growing around doorways.

Dried lavender, elderflowers or chips of cedar wood will
deter moths and scent your fabrics. Put some in linen or cotton bags
– which can be made from old handkerchieves – and place them in
wardrobes and drawers.

Trap wasps or bees with some sweet liquid in a tall glass jar, put
the lid on once they have entered and release them outside.

Deter silverfish by keeping surfaces dry. If they do appear,
sprinkle some dampened cloths with powdered plaster and leave
overnight on surfaces upon which the silverfish have been seen, before
shaking the cloth outside in the morning. Alternatively, put
a couple of cloves in drawers and cupboards.

Squirrels are a nuisance when they dig up bulbs from
window boxes and hanging baskets. Luckily they dislike
'cayenne hot' capsicum pepper, so sprinkle it on top of the soil
and on the window ledges to deter them.

Odour Prevention

**Fridges, bathrooms and bins can all smell a bit pungent,
especially in the summer months, but fortunately there are
many ways to avoid and combat the problem.**

The best way to stop your fridge smelling is to keep an eye
on the contents so they don't go rotten. Regular cleaning with a
solution of water and distilled vinegar will combat any existing smells
and give you the opportunity for a clear-out.

A jar filled with a 4:1 solution of cold water and bicarbonate
of soda at the back of your fridge will help to prevent smells.

To eliminate fridge odours, place half an apple, a lump
of charcoal, some slices of bread or some used coffee grounds
in an out-of-the-way corner.

Fridges sometimes smell because they're not shutting
properly. Test the seal by trapping a bank note in the door.
If you can pull it out, you need a new seal.

Remove fish odours from bins and surfaces by wiping with a
4:1 solution of water and bicarbonate of soda, or soda water.

To prevent the growth of bacteria and moulds which cause odours to
develop, sprinkle half a cup of borax in the bottom of your bin. For
maximum effectiveness, tip the old borax into the full bag and shake
fresh into the bottom of the bin each time you change the bag.

To help to deter insects as well as neutralize odours,
put a couple of mothballs in the bottom of your kitchen,
bathroom and wastepaper bins.

Do you have a waste-disposal unit in your sink that's become blocked and smelly? Try dropping ice cubes and orange or lemon peel down it, before flushing with cold water.

Pouring flat cola down your toilet bowl helps to shift limescale and prevents odours from building up.

To clean a toilet bowl, drop in a couple of effervescent stomach-upset tablets such as Alka Seltzer™, and leave for 30 minutes before brushing and flushing.

Distilled vinegar or soda water can be used to banish urine smells in the bathroom. Simply wipe the area with a cloth soaked in either substance. For long-term odour prevention, place an old yoghurt pot filled with cat litter in a corner.

Perfume and Potpourri

A sweetly-scented room is a pleasure to occupy and can enhance your sense of well-being, so here are some quick tips to freshen any space.

Dab a few drops of your favourite scent onto lightbulbs to ensure that rooms are flooded with light and fragrance every time you turn on the switch. Make sure the light has been off for a while before applying the perfume – otherwise the bulbs may shatter.

To get rid of lingering tobacco smoke, place a bowl containing 1 tablespoon of lavender oil and 1ml ammonia mixed with 500ml water in the room until the smell has gone.

Musty odours can be eliminated by regular airing, and, in the winter months, by placing citrus peel on warm radiators around the home.

Scented flowers such as gardenias or roses will fill a room
with their natural scent, so plant them near a window or have
vases of cut flowers in your rooms.

Freshen the air in your home easily and naturally by
mixing some lemon juice with water, putting it in a spray bottle
and misting rooms each day.

To make your bathroom smell nice, mix 10 drops of your
favourite essential oil with some baking powder, sprinkle on the
bathroom mat, leave for an hour and then shake outside.

Make your own air-freshening tablets by mixing 125ml of salt,
125ml of flour and a few drops of essential oil together to form a
paste. Roll the paste into balls, using your hands, and leave to dry.
Place the dried balls in the corners of rooms.

Dusting and Polishing

Dust-free, polished woodwork and ornaments improve the look of any room. Here are some easy ways to tackle the worst marks and tarnishes.

Rub a water stain or scratch on woodwork with a shelled walnut to help fill and disguise it. Alternatively, stain the scratch with a little iodine and fill it in by rubbing the area with some high-quality beeswax.

Eliminating some white water or heat rings on wooden surfaces can be more difficult. If rubbing with a shelled walnut doesn't work, try rubbing the area with a 1:1 paste of baking soda and non-gel toothpaste followed by buffing with normal polish. Alternatively, you could try rubbing the area with a cloth dabbed with vegetable oil and then cigarette ash, or applying some real mayonnaise, leaving it overnight, and then wiping clean with a dry cloth.

Make sure that your duster is made from cotton or flannel because synthetics can scratch the surface of many items.

Fabric-softener sheets help to repel dust so use one to wipe down the slats of your blinds after dusting.

To dust delicate items such as lampshades and ornaments, use a soft paintbrush. It will enable you to access all the nooks and crannies gently.

Televisions and electrical equipment become dusty very quickly because they produce static electricity and that attracts dust molecules. To combat the problem, wipe the item with a rag moistened with a 1:4 fabric conditioner and water solution, or use a fabric softening sheet.

You can dust hard-to-reach, narrow areas, such as
between a book shelf and a wall, by sliding a sock over the
end of a hanger and using that to clean.

Shine as you dust by using a cloth that has been soaked
in a mixture of 1 litre of water, two tablespoons of distilled vinegar
and four drops of lemon oil, before being wrung out. Once you
finish cleaning, keep the cloth in an jam jar with the lid
on to keep it moist.

Make your own wood polish by adding a few drops of
lemon juice to a 3:1 mixture of olive oil and distilled vinegar.
Apply to wooden surfaces with a sponge or mop according
to the area to be covered.

For brilliant brass, rub the article with half a lemon which has been dipped with salt. This cleans and shines in one.

To clean heavily tarnished silverware, bring
2 teaspoons of salt, 2 teaspoons of bicarbonate of soda and 1 litre
of water to the boil in a pan with a piece of aluminium foil in
the bottom. Then place the silverware in the liquid, boil for
3 minutes and dry and polish with a soft cloth.

Glistening Glass

Smudged, dirty glass and mirrors are a real letdown, especially if they are on display, so here are some top tips to make them shine.

Crystal should always be handwashed – never put it in the dishwasher. For an extra-clean gleam, wash it in a 1:3 solution of distilled vinegar and water.

To clean glass vases and remove the odour which flower stems can sometimes produce, half fill them with cold water, add a tablespoon of mustard powder, stir and leave for 30 minutes before rinsing.

Air freshener is a great alternative to window cleaner for cleaning mirrors, and it makes it smell fresh too.

Fill scratches on mirrors with a paste of non-gel toothpaste and silver polish, leave for 5 minutes and then buff off with a lint-free cloth.

For streak-free mirrors and glass surfaces, try using a solution of water and ammonia in a dilution of 10:1 and wiping with old newspaper.

To remove all traces of grime from a glass container, half fill it with water, add some peeled and grated potato and leave to soak for as long as possible. Alternatively, add a dash of vinegar, a handful of uncooked rice and a pinch of salt to the water in your container and swirl it around before rinsing.

Unused coffee filters are great for cleaning glass ornaments
and windows because they don't leave streaks.

When cleaning glass-fronted pictures, always spray
the cleaning solution onto the cloth rather than the glass itself, as
drips from direct spraying may seep under the
glass and spoil the picture.

Tiles and Taps

**Hard water and limescale can leave bathroom fixtures
and fittings dull and scaly, or, at worst, mildewed and slimy.
While there is no permanent solution, there are ways to
produce that clean sheen every time.**

A dampened cloth sprinkled with bicarbonate of soda
works wonders on porcelain tiles and sinks.

Shift rust and water spots on stainless-steel taps and fittings by
rubbing with lighter fuel or distilled vinegar.

For a lasting shine on dirty brass fittings, smear with brown
sauce and then polish with a cut lemon dipped in salt. Alternatively,
rub with a cloth dampened with white spirit.

Has your white bath become dull and marked with age?
Mix some turpentine with a teaspoon of salt and wipe it over
the whole surface before rinsing well with warm water.

Lift yellow stains underneath taps by applying a paste made of equal
amounts of salt and distilled vinegar. Leave it to work for 30 minutes.

Use a mixture of liquid laundry detergent and water to
clean the grime from bathtubs and tiles. It will also restore the
original brightness to tiles discoloured by hard water.

Baby oil acts as a barrier against limescale and soap scum when
rubbed onto wall tiles and shower screens (not the floor) after
each cleaning, keeping them cleaner for longer. Alternatively, keep
a spray bottle containing a 1:5 solution of bleach and water in the
bathroom and spray the tiles and shower screen every day.

To remove the white marks left by hard water on a plastic shower
screen, rub with a used fabric-conditioner sheet.

Clean a shower curtain in the washing machine, adding laundry
detergent and a little diluted bleach – instead of fabric softener
– to the final rinse. Then dry, fully extended, on a washing line.

If you don't want to take your showerhead apart to unclog holes
encrusted with hard-water scale, fill a plastic bag (making sure it has
no leaks) with distilled vinegar, submerge the shower head in the
liquid, secure the bag with an elastic band and leave overnight.

Banish mould and mildew and restore grouting to its former
whiteness by pressing paper towels soaked in bleach onto the
affected areas and leaving for as long as possible.

Soak tiles in neat distilled vinegar for 10 minutes to help
clean away hard-water marks.

Rejuvenate and polish tired tiles and whiten grouting by
spreading a thin paste of powdered wall filler and water over the area
and leaving for 30 minutes before rinsing off.

To clean enamel fixtures quickly, rub with a cut lemon.

Drains, Plugholes and Pipes

Blocked plugholes and drains have all too predictable consequences. These environmentally friendly suggestions offer simple ways to avoid, and solve, inefficient drainage and that tell-tale smell.

To prevent drains and pipes becoming blocked,
make a habit of liberally coating the drain area or plughole with
bicarbonate of soda and then rinsing with boiling water. Do it at least
twice a month for best results.

If a drain is blocked, pour 2 tablespoons
of bicarbonate of soda and 2 tablespoons of distilled vinegar
down the plughole, putting the plug in while the mixture fizzes.
Then rinse with boiling water, and, if necessary, use a plunger.

Invest in plug strainers to prevent food remnants and hair
going down the plughole and blocking the pipes.

Effervescent tablets for upset stomachs work wonders on blocked
drains or plugholes. Simply crumble a couple into the hole before
rinsing through with distilled vinegar, waiting a few minutes
and then rinsing again, this time with boiling water.

Rinsing coffee grounds down the plughole helps to unclog blockages
in the short term; tea leaves will cause a blockage.

Tip the boiling water used to cook potatoes down an outside
drain – it will help to shift any lingering waste.

Windows and Window Frames

Dirty windows, frames and ledges all detract from the look of a room. These labour-saving suggestions will take much of the pain out of cleaning them.

Wash windows with the water left over from boiling potatoes, as it leaves them gleaming. Alternatively, use a distilled vinegar and water solution in a ratio of 10:1 to clean both windows and painted window frames.

If you don't have time to wash the windows, remove grease marks with turpentine before rubbing the glass with old newspaper.

Coat the window frame and sill with clear silicone floor polish as this will deter dust from settling.

DIY

Do your dabbles in DIY end in tears, wonky lines and

spilled paint? Is your toolbox a disaster zone? If so, then take a peek

at these trade secrets and discover how the professionals

make it all look so easy.

Painting and Decorating

Painters and decorators can be very expensive, and many people prefer to have a go themselves. Here are some fool-proof tips to ensure and maintain a professional finish.

Are you having trouble removing remnants of old wallpaper? Once you have removed the top layer, spray it with distilled vinegar and leave for a few minutes. Scrape off the excess glue and then wipe off the remainder with more vinegar before rinsing with water.

To get rid of crayon marks on painted walls and paintwork, dip a dampened rag into baking soda and rub over the area. Alternatively, a thin application of spray lubricant removes all traces of crayon from painted walls, and can be rinsed off with soap and water.

If the paint is bobbling and flaking on a windowsill, water is probably getting in somewhere. Check the seals before stripping and repainting the affected woodwork.

To deter bugs and stop them sticking to the wet
paint when painting a room with the window open in summer,
add a few drops of insect repellent to the paint pot.

Line a paint tray with tin foil – it makes cleaning up at the
end of the day much easier.

Always stand a paint pot on newspaper or on
a paper plate if you are painting directly from the pot and
will need to move it around.

When painting the ceiling, cut a hole in a paper plate or
an old bath sponge and put it on your wrist to prevent drips
trickling down the paintbrush and onto your arm.

To achieve a clean, straight line when painting
cylindrical objects, such as chair and table legs, mark the level to
which you want to paint with a strip of masking tape around the
object and then paint up to the tape. When the paint is dry, remove
the tape and you'll be left with a neat finish.

If you lose the lid to your pot or need to cover some paint
which has been decanted into a smaller container during the day, use
an old shower cap or some cling film to cover the pot and
prevent the paint from drying out.

Avoid wasting paint if your brush is loaded at the end of
the day, or if you have to stop in the middle of painting, by wrapping
the brush in aluminium foil and putting it in the freezer. When you
need it again, simply take the brush out and leave it to defrost
before carrying on.

Place a dish of chopped onion in the room you are
decorating – it will help to get rid of paint fumes.

Look after your brushes. Clean as usual, rinse in water with a few
drops of fabric softener, and then secure the tip with an elastic band
when dry to keep the bristles in shape.

Transfer left-over paint into a smaller labelled tin, detailing the
manufacturer, colour and type. This way you have some on hand for
touch-ups and will be able to obtain more of the same colour
if you need it in the future.

Use a disposable razor to remove any paint that has spattered
onto the windows when painting sills.

Make sure you drill to the required depth
when putting up pictures or shelves by marking the drill bit
with a piece of masking tape.

Worried about banging your fingers when you hammer in a nail?
Try holding the nail steady with a wooden clothes peg rather than
your fingers for the first couple of blows.

To prevent your tools from rusting, place a moth ball in
the bottom of the tool box.

Keep small screws and nails tidy by sticking them
to a magnet.

Storecupboard Saviours

A well stocked storecupboard will give you the power to clean
with ease, so here are a few of the best and most frequently
used grime busters for tackling the task of everyday
household hygiene.

A-Z of Essentials
Indispensable ingredients for successful cleaning

Here are a few of the substances most commonly used in traditional household cleaning and stain removal. For safety, keep them away from children and pets, always follow instructions on the packet and handle with care.

Ammonia
Removes blood and fruit juice stains, and acts as a powerful cleaning agent. Gloves should always be worn when using this alkaline chemical, and good ventilation is essential.

Baby oil
Prevents grease building up on tiles and sinks and cleans stainless steel.

Banana skin
Great for cleaning shoes.

Bicarbonate of soda
Absorbs odours, cleans and is a gentle abrasive.

Biological washing detergent
Contains enzymes which break down protein and other stains.

Bleach
Multi-purpose disinfectant. Gloves should always be worn when using this liquid.

Borax
Natural deodorizer and disinfectant made from sodium, boron, oxygen and water. Gloves should be worn when using this powder.

Castor oil
Natural waterproofing agent.

Cat litter
Absorbs odours and liquids.

Chalk
Absorbs substances such as perspiration on collars.

Cinammon
Deters ants.

Distilled Vinegar — also known as *White Vinegar*
Can be used as fabric softener. Also is a disinfectant, neutralizes odours, removes limescale and grease and lifts stains.

Effervescent tablets for upset stomach
Dissolves and lifts grime.

Egg shell
Helps to brighten whites and make flowers last longer.

Glycerine
Softens and lifts numerous stains.

Ground coffee

Clears drains and lifts stains from dark-coloured carpets.

Hair shampoo

Gently cleans delicates such as cashmere.

Hairspray

Fixes stains such as ink and prevents them spreading.
Also deters flies and bees.

Hydrogen peroxide

Bleaching agent.

Lavender

Helps deter flying insects and perfumes laundry and rooms.

Lemon juice

Natural bleach and disinfectant.

Methylated spirits

Helps to dissolve stains.

Mint
Deters ants and mice.

Olive oil
Conditions leather.

Potato water
Brightens discoloured carpets, cleans glass and unblocks drains.

Rosemary
Deters insects.

Salt
Extremely absorbent and acts as a gentle abrasive
when cleaning.

Spray lubricant
Dissolves grease.

Talcum powder
Absorbent.

Tea leaves
Help to absorb odours.

Tea tree oil
Disinfectant.

Turpentine
Lifts paint stains.

Washing-up liquid
Concentrated soap which cuts through grease
and dirt and disinfects.

Temperature

To convert °Fahrenheit to °Celsius: (°F - 32) x 5/9 = °C
To convert °Celsius to °Fahrenheit: (°C x 9/5) + 32 = °F

°Celsius	°C or °F	°Fahrenheit
-23	-10	14
-18	0	32
-12	10	50
-7	20	68
-1	30	86
4	40	104
10	50	122
16	60	140
21	70	158
27	80	176

Length

1 inch = 2.540 centimetres	1 centimetre = 0.3937 inches
1 foot = 0.3048 metres	1 metre = 3.281 feet
1 yard = 0.9144 metres	1 metre = 1.094 yards

centimetres	cm or inches	inches
2.54	1	0.39
5.08	2	0.79
7.62	3	1.18
10.16	4	1.58
12.70	5	1.97
15.24	6	2.36
17.78	7	2.76
20.32	8	3.15
22.86	9	3.54
25.40	10	3.94

Distance

1 mile = 1.609 kilometres   1 kilometre = 0.6214 miles

kilometres	km or miles	miles
1.61	1	0.62
3.22	2	1.24
4.83	3	1.86
6.44	4	2.49
8.05	5	3.11
9.66	6	3.73
11.27	7	4.35
12.88	8	4.97
14.48	9	5.59
16.09	10	6.21

Speed

1 mile/hour = 1.6 km/hour
1 km/hour = 0.62 miles per hour

Area

1 sq inch = 6.452 sq cm	1 sq cm = 0.1550 sq inches
1 sq foot = 0.0929 sq m	1 sq m = 10.764 sq feet
1 sq yard = 0.8361 sq m	1 sq m = 1.196 sq yards
1 sq mile = 2.590 sq km	1 sq km = 0.3861 sq miles

Volume

1 cu inch = 16.39 cu cm	1 cu cm = 0.06102 cu inches
1 cu inch = 0.01639 l	1 cu m = 35.315 cu feet
1 cu foot = 0.02832 cu m	1 cu m = 1.308 cu yards
1 cu yard = 0.7645 cu m	1 l = 61.024 cu inches
1 gallon = 4.546 l	1 l = 0.219 gallons

1 US cup = 225ml
1 Australian cup = 250ml

Mass

1 ounce = 28.35 grams

1 pound = 0.4536 kilograms

1 ton = 1016.05 kilograms

1 gram = 0.03527 ounces

1 kilogram = 2.205 pounds

1 kilogram = 0.000984 tons

1 pound = 16 ounces

1 ton = 2000 pounds

1 kilogram = 1000 grams

Kilograms	Kg or Pounds	Pounds
0.45	1	2.21
0.91	2	4.41
1.36	3	6.61
1.81	4	8.82
2.27	5	11.02
2.72	6	13.23
3.18	7	15.43
3.63	8	17.64
4.08	9	19.84
4.54	10	22.05

International Dress Sizes

UK	Europe	US
6	36	8
8	38	10
10	40	12
12	42	14
14	44	16
16	46	18
18	48	20

International Children's Shoe Sizes

UK	Europe	US
6	23	7.5
7	24	8.5
8	26	9.5
9	27	10.5
10	28	11.5
11	29	12.5
12	31	13.5
13	32	1.5
1	33	2.5
2	34	3.5

International Women's Shoe Sizes

UK	Europe	US
3	35.5	4.5
4	37	5.5
5	38	6.5
6	39.5	7.5
7	40.5	8.5

International Men's Shoe Sizes

UK	Europe	US
6	39	6.5
7	41	7.5
8	42	8.5
9	43	9.5
10	44.5	11
11	46	12
12	47	13